Routem

The Last Eleven Months

by

John M Willis

Published by
John Willis

CONTENTS:

Front cover picture: RM5 at Clapton Garage, Hackney on the last day of Routemaster operation on route 38.

Frontispiece: One Routemaster from another in Regent Street

ISBN 0-9554216-0-8

Published by John Willis
2 Pwll y Waen, Ty'n y Groes,
Conwy LL32 8TQ

First Published 2006

Printed by Cambrian Printers,
Llanbadarn Road, Aberystwyth, SY23 3TN

Introduction

This book is a personal tribute to the Routemaster, a bus that is the last in a long line of successful buses, which have been beloved by the public who have travelled on them.

It does not argue for the continuation of the Routemaster in public service. Indeed sadly, all things, both good and bad come to an end eventually. In transport terms one could recall the passing of the trams, and the trolleybuses, both forms of transport that had their devotees. The Routemaster has of course been with us for over fifty years, and was in service constantly for 49 years. That means that a huge section of the travelling public, both in London, and elsewhere, remember it with affection, and nostalgia.

But inevitably its final day has come, and by the time you read this book, it will have passed from London's streets, with the exception of a few buses that will operate two heritage routes. Thanks to these, there will still be an opportunity to ride a Routemaster in London, at least for a little while yet.

This book then presents a number of photographs, taken by the author, of Routemasters doing what they do best, and what they were designed to do, that is operating as a service bus in Britain's Capital City, London. The photographs have all been taken during the last eleven months of 2005, the last year to see normal service routes operated by the Routemaster.

The photographs are mainly of everyday scenes of Routemasters going about their usual duties, and all were taken between early February 2005, and the final day of operation of Routemasters in normal service, on December 9th 2005. Some photographs have been included of 'special' buses which appeared at the last day 'celebrations' (if that is an appropriate word), on the various routes. On these days, it had become a tradition for some unusual, and often historic buses, to appear, and it seemed a shame to exclude these photographs, but they are in the minority. Also included is the occasional photograph, (usually no more than one for each route), of the vehicles replacing the Routemasters.

Routes covered include, in order of the disappearance of their Routemasters; route 19 from Finsbury Park to Battersea Bridge; route 14, from Tottenham Court Road Station, to Putney Heath; route 22, from Piccadilly Circus to Putney Common; route 13, from the Aldwych to Golders Green Station; route 38, from Victoria Station to Clapton Pond; and route 159 from Marble Arch to Streatham Station.

So the book then is essentially a farewell to a fine vehicle, which was the culmination of research and development carried out by London Transport, arguably the most successful operator of public service vehicles ever. It is also a last look at a style of transport which is historically as important as the Trams, and the Trolleybuses. (contd. on p 4)

(contd from p.3)
For decades bus passengers in Britain have been used to jumping on or off a bus, not only at official bus stops, but pretty well anywhere else where the bus was stationary. This facility had of course long vanished from most other parts of Britain, save London. It has been able to hang on in London because of the unique problems associated with the capital's traffic. There it had been long recognised that the open rear platform double-decker bus manned by a crew of two, was the most convenient and efficient way of moving the capital's bus using population.

The 'powers that be' obviously no longer feel that this is the case. Modern engine technology has presented the opportunity to fit clean engines, and advances in suspension can provide vehicles with low floors, enabling easier access for the elderly and disabled. Also the presence of doors reduces the likelihood of accidents. All these factors, together with the undeniable fact, that the Routemasters were wearing out, despite refurbishment, must inevitably have led to their eventual demise. It is also a fact that no one has ever been able to halt progress, but of course not all progress is good. It is tempting in the latter context, to think of the 18 metre long 'bendy bus' which seems to occupy an inordinate amount of road space, compared to the Routemaster, and which offers increased passenger capacity, only by failing to provide all passengers with seats.

One could argue that clean engines could be fitted to all Routemasters, as indeed they have to some already. Their lack of doors is an advantage in a city where it may take many minutes to cover those last yards to a bus stop. Passengers now have the frustration of standing behind closed doors, whilst the bus crawls through almost stationary traffic. They can at least gaze at the notice that tells them that the driver has specific instructions not to open the doors, other than at proper bus stops! Safety is of course important, but many generations of passengers have used the open rear platform bus, and survived. Or is it rather, as our society becomes more litigious, that the authorities become more cautious - or is it paranoid?

As far as low floors, and disabled access is concerned, it is difficult to see how the Routemaster could satisfy those needs. But surely man could design a vehicle that offers the Routemaster's advantages, plus those of accessibility. Sadly of course, there is no London Transport nowadays, to put in the necessary research effort.

Finally, it might be apposite to quote A.A.M. Durrant, onetime Chief Mechanical Engineer of London Transport's Road Services. He talks of the Routemaster being the result of a long line of research and development, started by the London General Omnibus Company, with the 'B' type bus, and culminating in the Routemaster. He also writes that 'The Routemaster was designed for a long and economical life, and as a result many Routemasters would have their expected lifetimes extended'. He wrote those words as a foreword in 'The Routemaster Bus' by Colin Curtis, Published by Midas Books in 1981, a quarter of a century ago. How right he was!

CHAPTER ONE - Route 19

This book begins its coverage in February of 2005, and at that time there were six routes still operated by Routemasters. The first of these to be surrendered to more modern buses was route 19. This route had a terminus at Battersea Bridge in the West, and in the East at Finsbury Park Station. The route was operated by Arriva and was served by an outstation at Battersea. The vehicles taking over from the Routemasters were Alexander bodied Volvo B7TLs bearing the classification letters VLA - (see photo on p 14).

RML2387 is seen below on the last day of Routemaster operation on route 19. The bus is picking up passengers at the Green Park stop in Piccadilly. Just visible on the other side of the road is the rear of RML2408 on route 38 headed for Clapton Pond. Route 38 would exchange its Routemasters for Mercedes 'bendy buses' finally on October 28th.

033a164mb

091M31&01M13TE

Above - RML2514 is seen here at Hyde Park Corner, at mid-day on the penultimate day of the use of Routemasters on route 19. The bus is en route from Battersea garage for its new home, having been sold to its new owner. Right: The photographer then encountered the very same bus some six weeks later, but in preservation, and kitted out again with destination blinds for route 19. It is seen here at the Llandudno Transport Extravaganza on May 13th. The bus behind is preserved RML2400.

029/1A/32m&034M30

Above; Arriva's RM29 picks up passengers in the glow of the afternoon sun at Hyde Park Corner on April 1st - the final day for Routemaster operation on route 19. The same bus is seen below, two days earlier, but this time in Piccadilly, outside Green Park Underground Station, heading again for Battersea, and following an unidentified RML operating on route 38. At this stage, Routemasters on route 38 still had until October 28th. before they were withdrawn. In fact route 38 would be the penultimate route to operate Routemasters in normal service, leaving only route 159 to carry the Routemaster banner.

072M31&144A1

Above: RM25 seen here in Sloane Street, is headed for Finsbury Park Station on route 19. It is March 31st. with just over 24 hours to go before Routemasters relinquish their hold on this route. Arriva's RM25 dressed in Great Northern livery, was destined to be one of the last Routemasters on the route, operating up until evening on April 1st. Right: RM875 is seen here, also in Sloane Street but bound for Battersea Bridge. It is early evening on April 1st., the last day for Routemasters to operate route 19. The bus just disappearing at the left hand edge of the photograph is RML2347 also on route 19

Above - RML2387 boards passengers in Shaftesbury Avenue, on a wet 30th March 2005. It was just two days before route 19 would lose its Routemasters on April 1st. Could there possibly be some significance in that date one wonders? Attempting to squeeze between RML2387 and the tour coach is A Volvo B7TL in the VP class, operated by Metroline on route 98, which was converted from Routemaster operation the previous March. Below RML2266 is on route 19, in Lower Regent Street, earlier in 2005, on February 9th. 045/M30/128/&/066F9

RM1280 (above) stops for passengers in Piccadilly and (below) Metrobus RML2317 operating as a guest bus picks up passengers at the same stop. Both buses are on route 19 on the last day of Routemaster operation on that route.
(012&024/A1/64m)

Above: Arriva's RML 2533 on route 19 & London General's RML2605 on route 22 are at Hyde Park Corner on the last day of Routemaster operation on route 19. Both buses glow in the afternoon sunshine. (021/A1/32m)

Left: RML2665 in Stagecoach livery and bearing the Routemaster 50 logo pulls away from the bus stop at Hyde Park Corner. The bus is operating as a guest bus on route 19, on the final day of Routemaster operation on that route.

(013/A1/32m)

The two buses on this page are both RMLs, and both are in Piccadilly working route 19 to Finsbury Park Station. Above is RML2452 whilst below is RML2536. The date is February 9th. and both vehicles will be withdrawn just over 6 weeks later. 063F9&030F9

035F9&065F9

Above; RML2266 is in Piccadilly working route 19 and heading for Finsbury Park Station, during February 2005. It is closely followed by RML2326 on route 38 and making for Clapton Pond. Below is another view of RML 2266 on route 19, looking very long as it turns into Lower Regent Street from Jermyn Street on its way to Battersea Bridge.

The Old & the New

The replacement buses put in an appearance several days before the Routemasters disappeared. New Volvo B7TL (VLA112) above, picks up passengers at the end of March at Green Park in Piccadilly. The bus behind is RML2593 on route 14.

In strong contrast is Cobham Bus Museum's STL2377, (left). Dating from 1937, it is seen near Green Park Underground Station in Piccadilly , carrying invited guests, on the last day of Routemaster service on route 19.

056m31&029a1/64mb

RML2452, (above) was another bus seen going out of service from Battersea, on March 31st., without blinds. Also in the picture is DW63 on route 137, heading for Oxford Circus. The photograph was taken at Hyde Park Corner.

On the left, RM871 is seen here on route 19 in Piccadilly, pulling away from the Green Park bus stop just a day before Routemasters were withdrawn from the route. The man running for the bus in the right hand of the picture at least has a sporting chance of catching the bus. Tomorrow it will be another story, as once those doors are closed, there will be no choice but to wait for the next bus.

094m31&067m31

Above; Craven RT1431 belonging to Ensign Bus, rounds Sloane Square as it puts in an appearance as a guest bus on the last day of Routemaster operation on route 19. The Craven RTs were built by the Sheffield firm of Cravens, and had a five bay body in contrast to the usual four bays of most members of the RT family. RT1431 was new in 1949, and only served in London until 1955.

Left; RML2272 is seen at the same spot in Sloane Square, later in the day, as it heads for Finsbury Park Station.

003a1&007a1/32mb

Above: Arriva's RM346, its smartness belying its many years in service, heads along Piccadilly, bound for Battersea Bridge, on route 19. It is April the 1st. and already the new buses are beginning to take over the route, leaving only five routes left operating Routemasters.
Right: Blue Triangle's RT3871, also on April 1st. but seen here in Sloane Street, plays a supporting role as it operates as a guest bus on route 19, on the last day of Routemaster operation on the route.

017a1/64&044a1/64mb

Left: Arriva's RML2574, bound for Finsbury Park Station on route 19, competes with a SAAB convertible for space as it races into Shaftesbury Avenue from Piccadilly Circus on a very wet day in late March.

047m30

Right; RML2524 in green 'Shillibeer' livery is seen opposite Green Park in Piccadilly on a dull wet March 30th.. With just two days of Routemaster operation remaining on route 19, this was one of the more unusual vehicles to be seen plying the route. The bus was originally intended to appear as one of the last Routemasters on the 19, but rumour has it a seized engine made that impossible.

038M30

Above: RM713 on the final day of Routemaster operation on route 19 pulls away from a bus stop in Sloane Street, on its way to Finsbury Park Station. The bus looks smart in overall red without advertisements to detract from its good looks. Right: RML2382 on the same day, enters Sloane Square on its way to Battersea Bridge. This bus looks more care-worn than RM713, and there appears to be slight accident damage around the offside rear mudguard. 038a1/64m&065a1/64m

CHAPTER TWO - Route 14

After the conversion of route 19 to Volvo B7TLs there then remained only five routes operating Routemasters. Just two of these ventured out into Western London, beyond Hyde Park Corner, and these were route 14 from Tottenham Court Road Underground Station to Putney Heath, and route 22 from Piccadilly Circus to Putney Common. Both these routes lost their Routemasters on the same day, Friday July 22nd. There is no reason therefore why route 14 should appear earlier in this book than route 22, other than the simple fact that numerically, route 14 comes first. Both routes were operated by London General from Putney Garage, and both their Western termini were in rather rural surroundings, at least for Central Area routes. This chapter then considers route 14, although often buses were allocated to either route, and certainly some of the guest buses, on the final day, appeared on both routes. The vehicles that replaced the Routemasters were Wright Eclipse bodied Volvo B7TLs in class WVL.

Below: RML2640 on route 14 leaves the Fulham Road behind as it approaches Putney Bridge, en route for Putney Heath . As with most of London General's vehicles this RML looks well presented. 6140005J14

Above: RML2612 eases itself into traffic at Hyde Park Corner, against a backdrop of several newer buses on the other side of Knightsbridge as it works route 14 towards Tottenham Court Road Station on April 1st. Below: RML2725 in mid June looks good with its cream centre band and large 'General' name on the bus side. It is approaching Putney Bridge, with All Saints Church Fulham in view to the left of picture. Note the chrome wheel nut guard rings, seldom seen by this date, which add a touch of style.
6140007j14&134a1/128mb

Above: RML2314 on route 14, heads towards Tottenham Court Road Station. The bus is at Hyde Park Corner on June 14, with some five weeks still left in service. Note the complete absence of advertising. Many Routemasters were stripped of their advertising in the last days of operation but this seems to have been done rather early in this case. Right: RML2345 on route 14, bound for Putney Heath, is seen here rounding Hyde Park Corner. (Note the cheaper hopper type windows - indicative of a refurbished body) - Alongside is VNL32265 of First operating route 10.

- 6140132j14&6140073j14

Above: RML2453 on route 14, boards passengers on the South Western end of Putney Bridge, in mid June with just over a month to go of Routemasters on route 14. The bus is heading East towards Tottenham Court Road Station. The large striking building visible to the left of the bus is the Putney Wharf Tower Building. Left: RML2680 on Route 14 leaves Piccadilly and enters Piccadilly Circus in early February, en route for Tottenham Court Rd Station - The bus is looking a little the worse for wear (unusual for London General) with some poorly matching paintwork, perhaps the result of an accident. 6140024 j14&028f9

Above: RML2321 on route 14, leaves Brompton Road and heads into Knightsbridge. It is mid June 2005 and the bus would normally terminate at Tottenham Court Road Station, but it will turn short at Piccadilly Circus.
Left: RML2398 is on route 14 in Piccadilly. The bus is heading for Putney Heath on the last day of March. Note the damage on the roof edge panels which has obviously been painted over. 6140063j14&060m31

Right: London General's RML2590 on route 14 boards passengers going East, at Hyde Park Corner on the last day of March 2005. Below, seen on the following day, also at Hyde Park Corner, but on the other side of the road, RML2453 on route 14, travelling West towards Putney Heath passes Arriva's RM5, operating route 19, but temporarily out of action, due to a breakdown. Both buses reflect the late afternoon sunshine

096m31128mb107a1128mb

Above: RML889, (now 214UXJ, originally registered WLT889), waits in traffic in Knightsbridge to enter Hyde Park Corner. Below RML2604 is at Hyde Park Corner. The bus is looking very smart in a new coat of red paint with a cream band, and its number in gold. It is also has a set of nut guard rings, very rare on RMLs at this time. Both buses are operating route 14 in mid June and are headed for Tottenham Court Rd Stn. CNV00009 (10A)&00007(8A)slrj14

Above & Right: RML2305 lays over at the Tottenham Court Road Underground Station terminus of route 14. The bus is in the deep shadow under the Centrepoint Tower.

As can be seen from the puddles, it was a very wet day when these photographs were taken, and the photographer was glad of the shelter provided by the buildings. It was mid June, and Routemasters had just over a month left to operate on route 14 by then. What a contrast there is between this city terminus and semi-rural Putney Heath at the other end of the route.

CNV00021 (23) &CNV00024 (25A)j15

Above RML2680 lays over at Tottenham Court Road Station, terminus of route 14, on a wet day in June. (Its garage plate, AF for Putney, is missing). The other Routemaster visible is RML2262, (which visited Toledo, Ohio, in November 1965). Below: a rear view shows both vehicles dwarfed by the Centrepoint Tower. In front of RML2680 is Metroline's TransBus Trident TPL293 6150003&6150005j15

Above: RML2422 was caught by the camera here as it drove onto Putney Bridge on June 14. The bus, which is nearing the end of its journey from Tottenham Court Road to Putney Heath, looks smart in a shiny new coat of paint, in spite of the dents to its nearside roof . Below: RML2371, is on route 14, heading West in Fulham High St, and about to approach Putney Bridge, bound for Putney Heath - CNV00016 (14A)slr9896j14&CNV00026 (24A)

Real value in an expensive world.
BEKO
14
PUTNEY HEATH
THE LION KING
ALDO
RML 2507
JJD 507D

DHL
14
PUTNEY HEATH
THEATRE ROYAL DRURY LANE
ALDO
CUV 321C

Above: RML2637 is on route 14, bound for Putney Heath on a gloomy wet day in mid June, that is brightened somewhat by the colourful nature of the surrounding theatre signs. The bus is in Shaftesbury Avenue, just outside the Lyric and Apollo theatres, giving passengers a chance to admire the architecture of this fascinating part of London, in the heart of Theatre Land. The area will be deprived of its Routemasters soon though as the only two remaining routes operating Routemasters and passing through Shaftesbury Avenue, the 14 and 38, will lose their Routemasters on July 22nd. and October 28th. respectively.

Facing Page top - RML2507 is seen here at Hyde Park Corner, operating route 14 in the late afternoon sunshine, which is shining straight up Knightsbridge and bathing the front of the bus in a warm glow, highlighting the red of the vehicle. Facing Page bottom - RML2321 is seen on the same day, also on route 14. It is in fact April 1st., the last day for Routemasters on route 19, and a little knot of photographers can be seen in the middle of the road, recording Routemasters while they still can. Both RML2507 & 2321 are headed West for Putney Heath, but it is worth noting the contrast between the two: RML2507 has the new type of hopper windows, indicating a refurbished body, whilst RML2321 has the original winding quarter drop windows.

6150023j15&124a1/128mb&128a1/128mb

Above: RML2371 is seen here rounding Hyde Park Corner, heading for Putney Heath. The bus, on route 14, seems to be providing motive power to someone on skates, (see the figure just near the rear platform of the Routemaster). Perhaps a little close to the wheels of the tour bus of the Big Bus Sightseeing Company for comfort - one slip.........! (There is another picture of RML2371 on page 29)

6140093 j14

Right: RML2314 pulls away from a bus stop on Putney Bridge, as it heads for the Putney Heath, terminus of route 14 on a bright day in mid June. There is another picture of this bus at Hyde Park Corner. on page 22.

6140031j14

Above: RML2422 looking good with excellent paintwork, and the bare minimum of dents on the roof edging panels is seen here in mid June at Hyde Park Corner, on route 14, and headed for Putney Garage. CNV00031 (31A) j14/9895

Right: RML2305 is seen here in New Oxford Street on route 14. The bus has been laying over at the Tottenham Court Road terminus (see p27) and is about to pick up passengers prior to starting its return journey to Putney Heath. The 'black' cab just disappearing from the picture on the offside of the bus, is anything but black, and adds a splash of colour in an otherwise dull and dreary June day.

6150016j14

Above: RML2578 rounds Hyde Park Corner on route 14, headed for Putney Heath. The bus looks very nearly as good as new in thc mid-day sun, and indeed appears to have a new coat of paint although it only has a few weeks left to serve on route 14. (Note the hopper windows, and compare them with the windows on the bus below). Right: RML899 is headed here along Piccadilly, on route 14, and bound for Putney Heath. The bus is registered 215UXJ - but originally it was WLT899.

CNV00030 (30A) slr9895j14 &CNV00014 (12A) slr9896j14

Pictured above is RML2570 on route 14, on July 7th., boarding passengers at the Hyde Park Corner end of Knightsbridge. The bus is heading for Putney Heath and was destined to be almost the last bus to be seen that day by the photographer. The entire bus and tube networks in central London were closed down on this day due to the terrorist bombings in Central London.

CNV00006(4A)010383slrjy7

Right: RML2520 has pulled out from its lay over position beneath the Centre point Tower, and is at the bus stop in New Oxford Street, to pick up passengers for its journey to Putney Heath. It is July 20 and Routemasters had only 48 hours left to serve this route when the photo was taken.
CNV00034 (32A)slr383jy20

By the time the above photo was taken, replacement buses had started to take over from the Routemasters. Below, taken the same day as the picture above, Wright bodied Volvo WVL30 on route 14 lays over near the Centre Point Tower waiting its turn to return to Putney Heath. CNV00026 (24A)slr383jy20

Above: RML2520 on route 14 lays over at Tottenham Court Road Station, in the shadow of the Centre Point Tower, with just two days to go before Routemasters are withdrawn from Route 14. The driver is in the process of climbing in and the bus will soon leave for distant Putney Heath. Below: Moments later RML2520 is in Charing Cross Road, bound for Putney Heath, having just left the shelter of the Centre Point Tower. Behind can be seen RM1968 on route 38, on its way to Clapton Pond.

CNV00037(35A)&CNV00028(26A)slr383jy20

Above - RML2297, replacement Wright Volvo WVL17, and RML2578 all operating route 14, lay over at the Putney Heath terminus, just two days before the cessation of Routemaster operation on that route.
Below: WVL17 and RML2578 both pull out of the bus lay over bay opposite the Green Man at Putney Heath. In this view it is possible to appreciate the length of the 30 foot long RML. Both buses are bound for Tottenham Court Road Station.
CNV00034(35)&CNV00036(37)slr385jy20

Above: RML2517 stands by the Green Man sign at the Putney Heath terminus of route 14, two days before the Wrightbus bodied Volvos took over the route. Below: Another view of RML2517 (furthest from camera), taken moments later, together with RML2578 (note the different type of windows on the two buses).
CNV00003(3)&CNV00007(7)slr386jy20

Above: RML2472 on route 14, looking in this picture almost as though it has just had a repaint, has just arrived at the Putney Heath terminus of route 14 two days before the last Routemasters were withdrawn from the route CNV00006 (6)slr386jy20

Right: RML2578 lays over at Putney Heath, terminus of route 14. The bus is hiding its registration number behind the grass at this semi-rural location as two enthusiast try to get a close up before the Routemasters disappear for ever. The rear of Wright Volvo WVL17 is just visible to the left of the shot.
CNV00035 (36) slr385jy20

The End of the Road

(July 22 - The last day for Routemasters on Route 14 Arrives)

Above: RMLs 2314 & 2305 lay over outside the Green Man pub, delightful semi-rural terminus of route 14. The buses were surrounded by enthusiasts who'd come to give their beloved Routemasters a grand send off. So many were there that their cars stretched as far as the eye could see along the edges of the roads across Putney Heath, and an enormous number arrived too by bus. Below: Blue Triangle's RTW75 as a 'last day special' at the Putney Heath terminus of route 14.

P60-7220032jy22 &P82-7220061a

Above: RML2606 speeds down Putney Hill, in the late afternoon on the last day of Routemaster operation on route 14. Below: RML2520 is seen here in Putney High Street on the same day, heading for Tottenham Court Road Station and followed by a Wrightbus bodied Volvo on route 85. P71-7220045ajy22 &P70-7220044A

Above: Also seen in Putney High St., opposite Ye Olde Spotted Horse, on the last day of Routemaster operation on route 14, is RML887. The bus is looking very smart, as it was repainted in traditional London General Omnibus Company Livery only a month previously. The bus which will be retained by London General for their private hire fleet, is on its way to Putney Heath) CNV00024(25)slr389jy22

To the right is another view of RML887 opposite the Green Man pub, as it arrives at Putney Heath, where it will lay over prior to returning to Tottenham Court Road Station. Originally registered WLT887, this registration number was sold and the bus re-registered 202UXJ. The bus had an Iveco engine fitted in 1990, but the vehicle at present has a Cummins engine.
P41-7220010jy22

Above: Cobham's 1937 STL2377 is at Putney Heath as a guest bus while below RML2673, RT1702 and WVL52 lay over at Putney Heath. Together the two photographs represent four generations of London buses to serve route 14. Three of them were designed and built by AEC for London Transport, sadly neither exists today. Sadly too, the Routemaster will be seen on route 14 no more after this day. Will the children on the upper deck of WVL52 attend a send off for these buses in a few years time?

P3-7220040jy22&CNV00009(10)slr384jy22

Above: Perhaps one of the most unusual guests on the final day was modernised Green Line Coach RF48, seen here turning into the bus bay opposite the Green Man at Putney Heath. Although this is the terminus for route 14 the vehicle carried route 22 numbers with a spurious destination, (at least for the present route 22) with side destination boards for route 706 P31-7220071 jy22

Right: This final photograph of the last day of Routemasters on route 14 shows Craven RT1431, owned by Ensign Bus and RML2578, (at one time based at New Cross Garage with London Central) at the Putney Heath terminus of route 14. As with all of Ensign's fleet, the RT looks very smart, as too does the Routemaster.
P407220009jy22

CHAPTER THREE - Route 22

The remaining route still serving areas of London West of Hyde Park Corner with Routemasters during July was route 22. It was not of course 'remaining' other than in the context of this book, as it lost its Routemasters on July 22nd., as did route 14. (Strictly speaking the last Routemasters on route 22 ran from Piccadilly Circus just after midnight but to all intents and purposes July 22nd., was the final day).

Route 14 joined up with route 22 at the top of Lower Regent Street. From there both routes passed through Piccadilly Circus, along Piccadilly, then down Knightsbridge. They then went their separate ways at Knightsbridge Station, buses on the 22 turning down Sloane Street, whilst those on route 14 continued along the Brompton Road. The two routes then came together again just before Putney Bridge, buses sharing their journeys briefly across Putney Bridge, to separate again immediately at the South Western end of the Bridge, the 14 going along Putney High Street, and thence to Putney Heath, whilst buses on the 22 made their way to Putney Common.

As a result, buses on both routes could be viewed in the rather attractive surroundings of Putney Bridge. This meant that a large number of enthusiasts congregated on and near the bridge to bid farewell to their Routemasters. Both routes were of course operated by London General from Putney Garage, and as a result the occasional bus on route 22 could also be seen in Putney High Street, heading for the garage. As with route 14, the vehicles that replaced the Routemasters were Wright Eclipse bodied Volvo B7TLs in class WVL.

Right: RML2361 on route 22 waits for traffic lights to change in Piccadilly during February. The bus had only a short distance to travel before it reached its terminus at Piccadilly Circus. It would then lay over in Lower Regent Street, until the time came to return to Putney Common.

060-P2090218f9

Above: RML2618, (alongside Metroline's TransBus Trident TP368), is in Lower Regent Street, making its way to Piccadilly Circus to pick up passengers for Putney Common. Below: RML2626 &2673 (both on route 22) lay over at the bottom of Lower Regent Street. Both photographs were taken during February. 071-P2090229f9) &020 - P2060168f9

Above: Another view of RML2626 in front and RML2673 behind, on route 22, laying over in Lower Regent Street in early February. The photograph also affords a glimpse of the rather splendid Victorian Italianate architecture in Waterloo Place and the Duke of York's column . The bus 'stop' tells potential passengers that this is a Bus Stand and that buses do not pick up passengers here. 019-P2090167f9

Right: RML2578 in this picture is on route 22 in Piccadilly at the end of March. This photo seems to emphasise the length of the bus, which has a refurbished body with hopper windows. 058m31

Above: Three RMLs in Piccadilly at the end of March. - RML2472 on route 22 heads West for Putney Common, whilst RML2578 on 22 heads East towards the nearby terminus of Piccadilly Circus. Following RML2472 is RML2398 on route 14, heading for Putney Heath. It is notable that no other bus types are visible in this shot in busy Piccadilly - a picture that couldn't be taken for much longer!

059m31

Right: RML2318 operating on route 22, on the last day of March, is seen here pulling away from the bus stop at Hyde Park Corner, and edging into the traffic in busy Knightsbridge. (note its hopper windows).

079m31

Above: RML899 is on route 22 on April 1st., at Hyde Park Corner. It is lit by late afternoon sun. 215UXJ is not the bus's original registration number - it was WLT899. (There is a photograph of this bus operating route 14 on page 34). The poster on the end of the bus shelter refers to a television programme on ITV.118/128m/al

Right: RML2371 on route 22 boards passengers travelling towards central London, in Knightsbridge at the Hyde Park Corner bus stop. The bus partly visible to the left of RML2371 is RML2514 belonging to Arriva, previously used on route 19, and just sold out of service and travelling from Battersea Garage, without destination blinds, en route for its new home, (see also page 6).

090m31

Above: Also seen on April 1st., at Hyde Park Corner, lit up by the late afternoon sun, was RML2305, operating route 22. (This bus can also be seen on route 14 on page 27). 119al

Right: RML2615 is also seen here on route 22 at Hyde Park Corner on April 1st. The man in the middle of the road is a photographer taking shots on the last day of Routemaster operations on route 19.
123al

Above: RML2578 on route 22 is at the bottom of Sloane Street, heading for Putney Common, whilst below, RML2520 on route 22 is at Hyde Park Corner, heading for Piccadilly Circus. Both pictures were taken in early April. 60/64m/a1&133/128mb

Above: RML2693 is seen here operating route 22 in Knightsbridge, near Hyde Park Corner, for London General.
Below: RML2605 is also operating route 22 at the same spot. Both photographs were taken in early April, and both buses were headed for Putney Common, with just over two and a half months left for Routemasters on this route.

023&022/32mb/a1

Above: RML2593 is seen here in mid June at Hyde Park Corner, operating route 22 and bound for Piccadilly Circus. The Arriva bus on route 137 to the nearside of the Routemaster is DW56, (a VDL DB205LF - Wright Pulsar Gemini). 6140119j14
Below: RML2732 on route 22 in June, pulls away from the bus stop near All Saints Church Fulham, at the North East end of Putney Bridge. CNV00006 (6A) slrslr9895j14

Above: RML2637 rounds Hyde Park Corner in June, en route for Putney Common. (Also visible in the picture is an unidentified RML on route 38, Green Line Coach W369XKL on route 757 for Luton Airport, plus a coach operating for Redwing and a police car, all at the traffic lights at the top of Grosvenor Place). Below: RML2543 on route 22 is at the top of Sloane Street, in mid June, as it starts to make the complicated turn into Knightsbridge, (involving first a left turn, then a 180 degree turn right), before continuing its journey towards Piccadilly Circus

CNV00033(33A)slr9895j14CNV00022(22A)9895slrj14

Above: RML2631 pulls away from the stop on the Lower Richmond Road, Putney, after a crew change. The bus is en route for Piccadilly Circus, and is operating route 22 in mid June, with just over a month before the Routemasters will be seen no more in this pleasant environment.
CNV00002(2A)slr9895j14

Right: RML2290 rounds a busy Hyde Park Corner whilst working the 22 route to Putney Common in the middle of June 2005 with about five weeks to go before the Routemasters cease operations on this route.
CNV00028 (28a)slr9895j14

Above: RML2637 on route 22 approaches Putney Bridge from Fulham, en route for Putney Common. Below: RML2605 queues in traffic on Putney Bridge, as it waits to turn right onto Lower Richmond Road, en route for Putney Common, the end of the 22 route. The conductor looks very relaxed as he enjoys the fine day in mid June, when both photos were taken. 6140003&6140030j14

Left: RML2637 on route 22 completes the complicated 180 degrees turn involved when leaving Sloane Street and entering Knightsbridge. Below: The same bus is seen moments later as it enters Knightsbridge and heads towards the Piccadilly Circus terminus of route 22. Both photographs were taken in June.

6140065&6140066j14

Above: RML2618, on route 22, leaves Fulham behind, as it moves onto Putney Bridge heading for the terminus at Putney Common. It is mid June with just over a month before Routemasters cease to operate here. 6140034j14

Right: RML2593, on route 22, waits at the traffic lights on Putney Bridge Approach, as it leaves Fulham behind, and heads towards the Bridge and the terminus at Putney Common. The photograph was taken in the middle of June.

6140032j14

Above: RML2568 on route 22 passes the Majestic Wine Warehouse, and the entrance to Putney Bridge Station, on the New Kings Road, Fulham. The bus is on route 22 headed for Putney Common, and is followed by a Dennis Dart (LDP132), headed for Putney Heath. Below - RML2520 on route 22, is at the same spot. Both photographs were taken in mid June. CNV00023 (21A)& CNV00019 (17A)slr9896j14

Above: RML2605 seen here just outside All Saint's Church Fulham, takes the right turn from Putney Bridge, (visible on the left of the photo.), into the New Kings Rd Fulham, as it heads East on its journey on route 22 to Piccadilly Circus. Below: RML2593 on route 22 approaches a bus stop on Putney Bridge. It will embark passengers here for its journey towards Piccadilly Circus. Both pictures were captured in mid June. CNV00021(19A) &CNV00028(26A)slr9896j14

Above: RML2441 on route 22, headed for Piccadilly Circus, follows RML2626 on route 14 headed for Tottenham Court Road through the Hyde Park Corner complex in June. Below: A replacement Volvo is already on the road in July, before the final day of July 22. WVL54 is seen here in Sloane Street.

CNV00001(2A)slr9897j14 & P7200101j20

Above: RML2297 is in Sloane Street, at the same spot as WVL54 on the facing page, a couple of days before Routemasters were withdrawn from route 22. P7200099j20

Right: RML2669 lays over at the Putney Common terminus of route 22 in a leafy spot where the bus crew can benefit from some shade on this hot July day. There were just two days left of service by the Routemasters here when this photo was taken. P7200045j20

Above: RML2297 squeezes between RML2605 and a scooter at the Putney Common terminus of route 22, as it pulls out to start its journey back to Piccadilly Circus on July 20, with just two days left of Routemaster service to Putney Common.

P7200062jy20

Right: RML2640 on route 22 lays over in Lower Regent Street. Although the bus does not pick up passengers at this point, the destination indicator has already been changed to show Putney Common. About to pass RML2640 is Arriva's RM1975, operating route 159 from Streatham Station to Marble Arch. Route 159 would be the last normal route operated by Routemasters and would not lose them until December 9th.

CNV00014 (15)slr385jy20

Above: RML2590 lays over in Lower Regent Street on route 22. It is waiting to return to Putney Common, although the destination blind still reads Piccadilly Circus. There is also a photograph of this bus on page 25, on route 14. Below: RML2669 lays over at the other end of the route, at the leafy terminus of Putney Common. Also in the photo, RML2305, recently arrived, has just finished offloading passengers. Both photos were taken on July 20.
CNV00023(24)slr385jy20&CNV00008(7A)slr390jy20

Above: So what's wrong with the back of a bus - and here's two for the price of one! RML2305 pulls past RML2669, as it leaves the leafy Putney Common terminus of route 22, where both buses have been laying over. They look as though they are having a friendly chat don't they? CNV00011(10A)slr390jy20

Right:
This photograph too was taken just two days before the last Routemaster finally pulled away from Putney Common. The bus in the picture is RML2669. It is laying over at the Putney Common terminus of route 22.

CNV00006 (5A)slr390jy20

It's All Over for Route 22

(The last day for Routemasters on Route 22 Arrives)

Above: RML2669, surrounded by enthusiasts, lays over at the Putney Common terminus of route 22, on the last day of Routemaster operation on this route.
CNV00032 (32)slr387jy22

Right: RML2466 is seen here on Putney Bridge, heading for Piccadilly Circus on route 22, on the last day of Routemaster operation on this route. The building in the background behind the bus is Riverbank House.
CNV00012 (12)slr387jy22

Right: RML899 (old registration number was WLT899, but now re-registered 215UXJ), arrives at the Putney Common terminus of route 22, on the last day of Routemaster operation on this route. (see this bus also on page 34 operating route 14).

CNV00018 (18)slr387jy22

Below: The same bus as above, photographed shortly afterwards, pulls away from the Putney Common terminus of route 22, and heads for Piccadilly Circus.
CNV00025(25)slr387jy22

Above: Beautifully preserved RM9 arrives at the Putney Common terminus of route 22. Right RM9 passes Wright Volvo (WVL36), the class which replaces the Routemasters after this day.

CNV00016(17) &CNV00021(20)slr389jy22

Above: RML2631, turns onto Putney Bridge from Lower Richmond Road. It is en-route to Piccadilly Circus on this last day of Routemasters on the 22. The tower to the top left of the picture belongs to St. Mary's Church Putney. P69-7220043Ajy22

Right: RML2669, (previously based at Waterloo Garage), arrives at Putney Common on the last day that Routemasters will appear here. (The photo was taken from the top deck of another Routemaster) P68-7220042A -jy22

Above: London General's preserved RM9, looking very smart in London Transport livery is seen here at Putney Common. The destination indicator suggests it is going back to Putney Garage for a break. Right: RML2631 stands on lay over at the same spot as RM9 above. (Both photos were taken on July 22)

P64-7220038&P67-7220041Ajy22

CHAPTER FOUR - Route 13

After routes 14 and 22 had lost their Routemasters on July 22nd., the next route to go was route 13. This route was served by London Sovereign Ltd, (a London United Company). The route extended from a terminus at the Aldwych in Central London to Golders Green Station in the North West of London. The buses used on the route were primarily the RMs refurbished by Marshall's, with fully automatic gearboxes, and the newer style of hopper windows. Some of these were destined to go to the new operators of the two heritage routes.

(These turned out to be a short working of route 9, operated by First between the Aldwych, and the Albert Hall and a short 15, run by Stagecoach, between Tower Hill and Trafalgar Square).

Route 13 was served by a garage in Station Road Edgware, a little way removed from the Golders Green Station terminus of the route, with a garage code of BT.

The final day for Routemaster operation of route 13 was to be Friday October 31st. The buses replacing the Routemasters were 22 new Scania East Lancs. bodied OmniDekkas, carrying the classification letters SLE, although some appeared on the route prior to the last day.

Right: RM180 on route 13 lays over near the church of St. Mary Le Strand in February, after completing its journey from Golders Green to the Aldwych. The bus, refurbished by Marshall's for Transport for London, and leased to Sovereign certainly looks very smart, as did most of the vehicles on this route. A chat between the photographer, and one of the bus crews at this location revealed that there were hopes that the Routemasters might still have another year left to them. Sadly this was not to be the case!

073(P2090195)f9

Above: RM180 & RM121 lay over at the Aldwych whilst working route 13 in early February. As the photo was taken RM180 prepared to leave to return to Golders Green. The building beside the buses is the church of St.Mary-Le-Strand. Built by Gibbs in 1714-17 it now forms a traffic island in the Strand.

046(was P2090198)f9

Right: RM1018 is seen here outside Charing Cross Station in early February, whilst bound for Golders Green Station. on Route 13 - (note the hopper windows, seen on all the Marshall Refurbished buses)

054P2090209) f9

Above: RM121 is seen here in Regent Street operating on the 13, in early February, en route for the Aldwych. 042(P2090192)f9

Right: RM441 is seen here operating on route 13 in Lower Regent Street in early February, with still some eight months left for Routemasters on this route. The bus appears to have had a temporary repair to its nearside front wing with, apparently, Duck Tape.

018(P2090166)f9

Above: RM191 on route 13 lays over at the Aldwych in February, whilst it waits to return to Golders Green. The bus just visible behind RM191 is RM121, also on route 13. Below: RM121 is on route 13 in Lower Regent Street. The bus, in Sovereign's livery, is heading for Golders Green Station on a dreary wet June day. Alongside on route 94 is London United's TransBus Trident Alexander ALX400 (TLA18)

051(P2090203)f9&6150032j15

Above: RM2071 on route 13 is looking very smart in this shot. It was taken in Haymarket, in bright sunshine, during July 2005, just three months before withdrawal of RMs for this route was due to take place. One of the very long 'Bendy' buses, on route 12, can just be seen behind RM2071.

CNV00009(10)slr385jy20

Right: RML2734 on route 13, heads down Orchard Street, just prior to turning left into Oxford Street, on its way to the Aldwych . This bus was one of only five RMLs held by Sovereign to operate route 13.

P8260015au26

Above: RM1218 on route 13, pulls away from the Station Forecourt at Golders Green Station during August. It is en route for the Aldwych, in spite of its destination blind still reading erroneously 'Golders Green'. As it goes it passes Metroline's VP541 operating route 260. Below: RM1005 pulls out of Golders Green Station, as it heads off to the Aldwych, on a glorious sunny August day. Also in the picture is a Dennis Dart of Metroline on route 268, and a Volvo B7TL-Wrightbus Eclipse Gemini, (VLW48) on route 102. P8260013&P8260011au26

Above: RM1627 is seen here in Regent Street operating route 13 during September. The bus is headed for Golders Green Station, whilst another Routemaster also on route 13, and a 'bendy bus' on route 12 can be seen in the background.

P9260041sep26

Right: RM1005 is seen here in the Haymarket during September. The bus is bound for the Aldwych, on route 13, with just a short distance left to go, passing through Trafalgar Square, and along the Strand.

P9260009sep26

Above: RM931 is seen here waiting at traffic lights at the lower end of Regent Street in September, whilst operating on route 13. The bus is bound for the Aldwych, with just about a month left of Routemasters on this route. P9260048sep26

Left: RM2089 on route 13, hesitates briefly at the bottom of Haymarket, whilst it waits to make the left turn towards Trafalgar Square, as it heads for the Aldwych, during September.

P9260007sep26

Above: RM45 operates route 13 for Golders Green Station, in Regent Street, during September - a close look reveals that the bonnet number on the cab side makes it appear we are looking at RM5 - but that is not the case. Just behind RM45 is Mercedes Benz Citaro, (bendy bus) MAL65 operating route 12. P9260053sep26

Right:
The modern architecture vies with the old in the background of this shot, as RM121 waits at the pedestrian lights on the South side of Trafalgar Square. The bus is heading East on route 13, for the Aldwych, during late September.
IMG1275can/s26

Above: RML2734 is seen here laying over by the church of St.Mary-le-Strand, at the Aldwych terminus of route 13 during September. This is one of the very few RMLs operating on the 13, and is also not a refurbished vehicle. It thus has the original quarter drop winding windows, and is looking a little careworn. Note too the 'wonky' route number 13. IMG1216cansep26

Right: RM1933 on route 13 arrives at St.Mary-le-Strand at the Aldwych where it will lay over before returning to Golders Green Station. It is passing one of the Mercedes Citaro Fuel Cell Buses (ESQ64991) operating on route RV1. These vehicles use hydrogen as a fuel and produce only water as an exhaust. IMG1223cansep26

Above: RM1568 lays over by the church of St.Mary-le-Strand at the Aldwych.
Below: RM1913 waits in traffic behind a Trident of First, in the Strand. Both Routemasters were on route 13, and were photographed in late September.
IMG1231&1239cansep26

Above: RM329 enters Trafalgar Square from the Strand as it works route 13 towards Golders Green Station in late September. It is followed by single deck Man 11 190 Optare Vecta MV5 of London United. Below: RM1735 on route 13 passes through Trafalgar Square heading for the Aldwych, also in September.
IMG1242&1256cansep26

Right: RM1218 is seen here operating route 13 in early October. The bus is at the top of Regent Street and on its way to Golders Green Station.

img1337can0ct6

Below: A major diversion of route 13 between Swiss Cottage and Golders Green Station on October 6th., led to buses travelling via Cricklewood, Kilburn and the A5. The result was a severe shortage of buses at the central London end of the route, then bunching at Golders Green, as witnessed by this wonderful array of five Routemasters. In the picture at Golders Green Station are, RMs 1568, 191, 2089, 931 & 659.

Img1376can113ao6

Above: RM2089 heads a line of buses at the Golders Green Station terminus of route 13 on October 19th. Behind it is SLE30, an East Lancs bodied Scania OmniDekka, one of twenty two of the type due to take over from the Routemasters within a couple of days of this photo being taken. Bringing up the rear is RM1562. Below: Also on October 19, RML2734 pulls away from the bus stop opposite the Swiss Cottage. The 'wonky' number 13 has now almost disappeared from view and has been in this state for over a month. (see photo on page 81). IMG1526&IMG1510 can/o19

The end arrives for Route 13

(The final day for Routemasters on Route 13)

Above: RM324 has just left Golders Green Station, to return to the Aldwych on the last day of Routemasters on route 13

Right: RLH61 of Ensign Bus is seen here with a full load of enthusiasts, at Swiss Cottage, 'celebrating' the last day of Routemasters on route 13

IMG1893&1883can118/9o21

Left: RTW75 (of Blue Triangle) is seen here in the Strand, opposite the Strand Palace Hotel, operating as a 'special' guest bus during the last day of Routemasters on route 13

IMG1904can118/9o21

Right: A really venerable old lady, seen here on the last day of Routemaster operation on route 13, was Cobham's 1937 vintage STL2377. The bus is seen here, in bright sunlight, in the Finchley Road, near Swiss Cottage, and heading for Baker Street, with a number of invited guests.

IMG1844can118/9o21

Left: RM613 seen here at Swiss Cottage, looks very smart in London Transport livery, forthe last day of Routemasters on the 13

IMG1794can118/9o21

Above: ER880 lays over at the Aldwych on the last day of Routemasters on route 13. (ER was the designation given to the first lengthened Routemasters, but only the first four carried this lettering, the remainder being called RML). The bus is in London United livery but with added 'Routemaster 50' roundels. Below: RM613 in London Transport livery, and with halogen bulbs glowing, prepares to leave the Aldwych for the last time on the evening of October 21st. IMG1930&2049can119o21

CHAPTER FIVE - Route 38

Arguably, route 38 was the most important route to lose its Routemasters in the period covered by this book. Certainly it employed the most buses, around fifty being on the road normally on a daily basis, and it probably carried the most passengers of the routes covered in the eleven months with which this book is concerned. It also served a large main line station, which none of the other routes covered here did. With one terminus at Clapton Pond in the East and the other at Victoria Station in the West, it probably covered a more diverse range of areas, in social terms, than did many of the other routes covered by this book.

Unlike the two routes operating from Putney Garage, and the 13, which used primarily refurbished vehicles, many of the buses appearing on the 38 were looking a little tired, and often in need of painting, by the time the end came.

Buses on route 38 operated from Clapton Garage which was situated near to Hackney Central Station. The code for the garage was 'CT'. The buses which replaced the Routemasters were Mercedes Citaro Bendy buses, and carried the bonnet reference of MA.

Because of the nature of the new vehicles, Clapton Garage ceased to be used for housing buses on route 38, after the Routemasters had retired, and changes were also necessitated at Clapton Pond, where the usual bus stand, by the pond, where buses would lay over pending return to Victoria, ceased to be used.

Below: RML2685 seen in Lower Regent Street in February, was typical of many Routemasters on route 38 in these last months. Looking a little careworn and battered, and carrying the marketing slogan 'to and from Sadler's Wells' it was headed for Victoria Station. 023f9

Right: RM1640 is on the bus stand for route 38 at Victoria Station during March. The photographer happened to strike a moment when there were few pedestrians at what is such a normally busy spot.
Below: RML2359 enters Piccadilly Circus, from Piccadilly, on a February day working to Clapton Pond.

020/128/m30/310&26f9

Right: RML2597 operating on route 38 on a very wet day in late March, boards passengers in Piccadilly opposite Green Park Underground Station.
Below: - RM2122 on route 38 is in Piccadilly on the same very wet day as RML2597 above. Note the heavy misting on the inside of the upper deck windows, suggesting it is pretty humid upstairs. This is a refurbished RM judging by the hopper windows.
042&027m30/31

Above: RML2528 on route 38 passes the Shakespeare Public House, on the corner of Buckingham Palace Road, And Terminus Place, as it enters Victoria Station, the end of its journey from Clapton Pond. The bus is looking a little careworn but would be operational for nearly another seven months when this photograph was taken in early April.

Right: RML2457 is on route 38 in Piccadilly, at the beginning of April, and is heading for Victoria Station.

005&021/64mba1

Above: RML901 on route 38, rounds Hyde Park Corner. The bus carries a 'Not in Service' destination blind, and as it has come round the island from Piccadilly it is probably heading back to Clapton Garage, or has been turned to maybe start a short run, perhaps from Piccadilly Circus, or Tottenham Court Road Station. (Note the 'Bendy Bus' in the background to the offside of the RML)

CNV00035 (34A)slr9895j14

Right: RML1968 is at the same spot as RML901, above, as the bus rounds Hyde Park Corner headed for Clapton Pond. Note the hopper windows on this Marshall refurbished Routemaster. Both photos on this page were taken in June.

CNV00037 (37A) slr9895j14

Above: RML2315 is on route 38 and is in Piccadilly heading for Victoria Station. Right: RML2277 passes a vehicle on the Big Bus Tour of London, in Piccadilly. The RML is on route 38, and headed for Clapton Pond. Both photographs were taken in June.

CNV00012 (10A)&CNV00010 (8A)
slr9896j14

Above: RM1145 on route 38 in June, looking very smart in a new coat of paint, leaves Victoria and begins its journey to Clapton Pond (Note the hopper windows indicating this is a Marshall refurbished vehicle). CNV00006 (4A)slr9896j14

Right: RM652 stands at the front of a row of three RMs on route 38 in June at Victoria Station. The bus has been refurbished and in fact this bus has returned to service from private preservation, when it was know affectionately as 'Rodney the Routemaster' - CNV0007 (5A)slr9896j14

Above: RML2370, is heading for Clapton Bus Garage at Hackney. Below: RML2457 heads for Clapton Pond. Both buses are carrying full number and route details on their sides, together with publicity for the Sadler's Wells Ballet. Both buses were on route 38 and were photographed in mid June at Hyde Park Corner.

CNV00005(6A)&CNV00012 (13A) slr9897j14

Above: - RM652 is seen here during July operating on route 38, and about to turn out of Buckingham Palace Road, into Terminus Place, at Victoria Station. It seems strange to see so much foliage in central London, and in this case it is due to all the trees in Grosvenor Gardens.

CNV00010 (8A)slr383j7&20

Right: RM2050 operating a short working on route 38, in July, lays over at Tottenham Court Road Station under the Centrepoint Tower. The bus is waiting to return to Clapton Pond. Note the hopper windows on this bus, and on RM652 above.

CNV00022 (20A)slr383j7&20

Left: RML2359 on route 38, turns right into Jermyn Street from Haymarket, on a sunny July day, as it travels towards Victoria Station.

Below: A splendid line up at Clapton Garage, on a warm August day, in 2005, but sadly a wonderful sight not to be seen for too much longer. Visible from the left are: RMLs 2356, 2571, 2344, 2355, 2528 & 2434

slr385jy20cnv00018&P8260007au26

Right: RML2494 on route 38, makes the right turn from Mare St, into Graham Road, Hackney, having just started the long run to Victoria Station.

The picture was taken on a sunny day in late August, when the Routemasters operating on route 38 had just over two months left to serve.

P8260005au26

Below: RM652 is seen here operating route 38, in Balls Pond Road, Dalston, and following a skip lorry. It is headed for Victoria Station. This view clearly shows the Hopper Windows on this bus. 04A(5) slr976287au26

Above: RML2544 is seen here in Graham Road, Hackney as it squeezes down the side of stationary traffic to reach the bus stop. The bus is on route 38 on its way to the terminus at Clapton Pond . Both photos on this page were taken in August. 05A(6)slr976287au26

Right: RM1185, (a refurbished RM with hopper windows), is seen here in the narrow one-way part of Mare Street, just near the entrance to Clapton Garage. The bus is en route to Victoria Station.
14A(15)slr976287au26

Above: RML2492 on route 38 to Victoria Station, is in Mare Street, near the entrance to Clapton Garage in late August. The bus behind is Stagecoach's TransBus Trident (17829) working route 55 to Oxford Circus 15A(16)slr976287au26

Right: The photographer hopped on RML2492 in Mare Street, but had to get off in Shaftesbury Avenue, outside the Apollo Theatre, when the bus was turned short at Piccadilly Circus. The bus is seen in Shaftesbury Avenue after the destination blind was altered. 21(21)slr976287au26

Above: RM1185 overtakes RML2492 which has stopped in Shaftesbury Avenue to unload passengers as a result of being turned short here. Photo taken late August. (See also photos on page 101) 20(20)slr976287au26

Right: RML888 is also seen here in late August in Shaftesbury Avenue, just opposite the Apollo Theatre, as it travels route 38 towards Victoria Station. This bus carries on its sides the promotional information for Sadler's Wells.

22(22)slr976287au26

Above: RM1164 goes out of service in Pembury Road, Hackney (at the Junction of Dalston Lane & Amhurst Road). The bus is returning to Clapton Garage after completing a journey from Victoria to Clapton Pond during the morning rush hour, on a lovely late August day. 07a(8)slr298604au26

Right: RML2406 completes the turn from Amhurst Road into Dalston Lane, Hackney, whilst operating route 38 from Victoria Station to Clapton Pond, on a warm and sunny day in late August. There would be just two months of Routemaster operation left on the 38 when this photo was taken. 14A(15)slr298604au26

Right: RML2416 turns from Mare Street, Hackney, into Graham Road. The bus has just left Clapton Pond and is en route for Victoria Station on the 38 route in late August.
8Aslr298606au26

Below: One of the pleasures of Routemaster riding was sitting in the downstairs front near side seat, and watching the road ahead, whilst also watching the driver. This photo was taken on a dull October day from that seat on RML2050 which was in Charing Cross Road, approaching Cambridge Circus. The two Routemasters visible are, RMLs 2526 & 2416. IMG1328can113a/o6

Above: RML2597 is seen here on route 38 in Bloomsbury Square in early October, and bound for Clapton Pond IMG1296/112a/can/o6

Right: Also in Bloomsbury Square, on the same morning as RML2597 above, was RML2280, which was also heading for Clapton Pond on route 38. It is interesting to compare the two vehicles. RML2597 looks as though it has comparatively recently received a repaint, whereas RML2280 still bears the Sadlers Wells promotional livery, with route details on the bus side, plus it has a chromium grill surround. IMG1299/112a/can/o6

Right:
RML2528 pulls into the bus stop to pick up passengers in Bloomsbury Square on route 38 during early October. With only just over three weeks before Routemasters relinquish their hold on this route, Bloomsbury Square will soon be hosting 'bendy-buses' on the 38

IMG1292can112a/o6

Below: An offside view in Bloomsbury Square, this time of RML 888 on route 38 heading for Clapton Pond. This photo also taken in early October. IMG1303can133/o6

Above: RML2409 is in High Holborn on route 38, during October, heading for Victoria Station. The bus behind the Routemaster is Stagecoach's Trans Bus Trident with fleet no. 17827 on route 55 to Oxford Circus.

IMG1305can133/o6

Left: RML2401 is seen here also in High Holborn in early October on route 38 for Victoria Station. It is followed by Arriva's DAF DB250LF (fleet no. DLA303)

IMG1310 can113/o6

Above: RML2386 is in High Holborn en route for Victoria Station, whilst working the 38 during early October. The bus seems to have lost some of its side advertisement. The tube station just visible in the distance, behind the bus, is Holborn Station. Below: RML2346 on the 38 in Procter Street heads for High Holborn and then Victoria - two of Metroline's Volvo B7TLs make a backdrop, the leading one being VP564.

IMG1313&IMG1314can113a/o6

Above:
RML2304 is seen here in full frontal view in Procter Street on route 38 for Victoria Station.
Right:
RM2122 passes building operations on the corner of Theobalds Road and Drake Street as it works route 38 to Victoria Station.
Both photographs were taken in early October.
IMG1316&IMG1319can113a/o6

Above: RML2503, (a forty year old Routemaster), is heralded by a 'modern' buses arrival indicator, as it approaches a bus stop in Theobalds Road whilst on route 38 for Victoria Station in early October. IMG1323can113a/o6

Left: RM1776 takes the turn from Roseberry Avenue into St. John Street, Islington, as it heads for Clapton Bus Garage, in early October. The sign on the shop visible to the offside of the bus points the way to the nearby Sadlers Wells Theatre.
IMG1425can114a/o6

Above: RML2334 is laying over at Clapton Pond, (terminus of route 38), under the Weeping Willow, which almost gives it the feel of a riverside setting in West London. The bus behind it is RML2526, also operating route 38.
Below: RML2304 passes RML2503 at Clapton Pond, as it leaves to head back to Victoria Station. (Both photos were taken in October just a week before Routemasters gave way to the Bendy Buses on this busy route). IMG1970&IMG2000 can119/o21

Right: RM909 is in Islington heading for Clapton Pond on route 38.
Below: RML2325 is seen at the very busy Angel Islington, operating route 38 towards Victoria Station. It is followed by a TransBus Trident of Stagecoach (17796), an unidentified refurbished RM on route 38, and a Bendy Bus on route 73. Both photos on this page were taken in October
IMG1397can113a/o6 &IMG1458can114a/o6

Above: RML2492 is at pedestrian lights at the Angel Islington in October. This view shows off well the promotional livery for the Sadler's Wells Theatre, and the fact that it is served by route 38. The bus is heading for Victoria Station and seems to be carrying a fair load of passengers. IMG1402can114a/o6

Right: RML2287 makes the right turn from Mare Street Hackney, into Graham Road, in October, as it heads for Victoria Station on route 38. For some reason the intermediate destinations blind is blank. In the background RML2544 can be seen emerging from under Hackney Central Railway Bridge. The tower belongs to St. John's Church which stands just near Clapton Bus Garage.
IMG1614can/o19

Right: RML2325 is photographed here in Graham Road Hackney, in mid October, just over a week before Routemasters are withdrawn from route 38. The bus is bound for Victoria Station, in spite of its erroneous destination blind reading Clapton Pond. Note the 'wonky' nearside upstairs left front window, common on many Routemasters by this stage.
IMG1623can/o19

Below: RML2483 makes the right turn from Mare Street Hackney, into Graham Road, as it heads for Victoria Station during mid October with just a week left for Routemasters on route 38. The two other buses in the picture are on route 73, both are operated by Stagecoach, and both are TransBus Tridents. The one on the left is No. 17912, and the other is No. 17879. IMG1612can/o19

The Last Day for Route 38 Arrives

Left: This RT appeared In Wilton Road, outside Victoria Station, early on the last day of Routemaster operation on route 38. It is RT190, and it is carrying invited guests for this memorable but sad day.

IMG2100can120/o28

Below:- RML2750 carrying a good load, and surrounded by enthusiasts leaves Victoria Station forecourt on the last day of Routemaster operation on route 38.
IMG2097can120/o28

Right: A frequent visitor at last day celebrations is Ensign Bus's RT 4421, seen here in typical London Transport colours, but with Ensign's name in gold. The bus is seen here in Terminus Place at Victoria Station on the morning of the last day of Routemaster operation on route 38.
IMG2110can121/o28

Left: RML2315 stands at traffic lights in Victoria Street, having just left Victoria Station for Clapton Pond, on the last day of Routemasters on the 38. The vehicle visible to the nearside of the Routemaster is a President of East Thames Buses on route 185

. IMG2114can121/o28

Right: TD895 - a Bristol K of Ensign Bus is in Lower Grosvenor Place. The bus is acting as a guest bus at the last day 'celebrations'. This vehicle actually worked the streets of London in the early 1950s. It is a former Tilling Group bus which was amongst several hired by London Transport to help with vehicle shortages.
IMG2121can121/o28

Above: A Truly Venerable Old Lady - ST922 is seen here in Balls Pond Road. Appearing by courtesy of Cobham Bus Museum, it did not operate a service on the 38, but carried invited guests, as part of the last day 'celebrations'. The ST - an AEC Regent, with a petrol engine and outside staircase, was first operated by Thomas Tilling, and is the same bus that operated heritage route 100 in the 1970s.
IMG2348can512crd/o28

Right: Arriva's RM6 in Golden Jubilee livery is seen here in Essex Road, Dalston on the final day of Routemaster operation on route 38. The bus just visible in the photo, and about to overtake RM6 is RML2344.

IMG2392can512crd/123/o28

Above: RML1650, (or as numbered here SRM3). The bus was renumbered, (being one of a group of twenty five numbered from SRM 1 to 24), in 1977, when it was painted into a silver livery for The Queen's Silver Jubilee celebrations. Later the vehicle spent time with Blackpool Transport and in 1997 it went for a while to Reading Mainline. Later it was bought by Transport for London, and refurbished by Marshalls, hence the hopper windows which can be seen in the photograph. It appears here as part of the last day 'celebrations' for Routemasters on route 38, in the Silver Jubilee livery and carrying the number SRM3.

IMG2388can512crd/123/o28

Right: RT1431, the ever popular Craven RT belonging to Ensign Bus, is seen here at the junction of Theobalds Road, and Grays Inn Road, headed for the Clapton Pond terminus of route 38, loaded to the gunwales with enthusiasts.

IMG2492can512crd/124/o28

Right: RML2328 is approaching the bus stop at the lower end of Roseberry Avenue, near the junction with Theobalds Road in the late afternoon of the last day of Routemaster operation on the 38. (See also the photograph below)

Img2494/can512crd/124/o28

Above: It is sometimes suggested that the people who are enthusiastic about Routemasters are simply old blokes who wear anoraks. The above photo gives the lie to this belief. It was taken on RML2328 on the last day of Routemaster operation on route 38.

IMG2496can512crd/124/o28

Above: RML888 is seen here in Balls Pond Road, on the final day of Routemaster operations on route 38. It is followed by Ensign's Craven RT - RT1431, which was taking part in the day's celebrations as a guest bus, (see also opposite page).

IMG2362can512crd123/o28

Above: RLH61 outside the entrance to Clapton Garage, Hackney. This beautiful low bridge AEC was operating as a 'last day' guest bus, courtesy of Ensign Bus. The vehicle has a sunken gangway on the right, meaning mind your head below. It also has a similar engine and preselector gearbox to those on the RT, so at a pinch it could be called a low bridge RT! IMG2287can512crd/122/o28

Below: RML2688, looking a little tired, together with refurbished RMs 2060 & 2122 offer a farewell parade at Clapton Garage on the last day. IMG2324can512crd/123/o28

CHAPTER SIX - Route 159

At one time route 159 had served Croydon, and vehicles operating the route were once based at Streatham Garage. That is history however, and latterly, under the Arriva umbrella, the route was served by Brixton Garage, (Garage Code BN), and it extended from Streatham Station in the South East, to Marble Arch in the North West.

After the demise of routes 13 and 38, both of which lost their Routemasters in late October, the 159 was the only place to see Routemasters, until the new Heritage Routes commenced operation on November 14th. These however utilised only about a dozen buses, and could hardly be called representative.

The 159 however, carried the flag for Routemasters until they were withdrawn from this route too on Friday December 9th. With their passing came the end of almost fifty years of Routemasters on the streets of London.

They had given sterling service, and many people felt they should have been allowed to go on for some years still. The arguments for and against their retention are many, and this is not the place to pursue them. Suffice it to say that all true bus lovers will regret their passing, and will miss their presence, and the ease of boarding and alighting associated with all open rear platform buses.

Although the final day for Routemaster service on the 159 was Friday December 9th., because of the busy road on which Brixton Garage was located, Routemaster service did not continue until late evening, but ended at around 2.30 pm. Guest buses too, in the main appeared on the penultimate day, December 8th.

Left: RML892 & RML2521 stand in the entrance to Brixton Garage in early February. RML2521 was to be the last Routemaster that the photographer rode on, on the final day of December 9th. It is easily recognisable due to the graffiti word 'Zeno' which appeared just below the destination indicator, which reads 'Out of Service'

005f9

Above: RM1124 waits outside Brixton Garage in early February. The two buses visible in the background are RML892 & RML2521. Below: RML2573 awaits its crew, before proceeding to Streatham Station.
007&004f9

Above: RML 2572 on route 159 queues in traffic in Lower Regent Street. The damaged roof edge panels on this vehicle have obviously been painted over without any attempt at repair. It is followed by a Dennis Trident (TA19) of Travel London, on route 3. Right. RML2366 is on the 159 in Lower Regent Street in February. Another RML on the 159 can be seen behind.

058f9&067f9

Above: RML2726 is seen here on route 159 in Streatham on a dull wet February day, heading for distant Marble Arch. Below: RML2521 stands 'out of service' in the entrance to Brixton Garage on a dull day in February. 002&006f10

Right: RM1292 is seen here in July at the traffic lights on Streatham High Road, outside Streatham Hill Station, just a few minutes into its long journey to Marble Arch. The bus looks smart and well cared for, and at this time had a little over four months left in service on route 159. P7210006jy21

Below: RML2264 & RM85 lay over in July, outside the old Streatham Bus Garage, the Streatham Station terminal point for route 159. They are in company with a Dennis Trident Alexander of Travel London, operating route 60. P7210012jy21

Right: RM85 turns across the Streatham High Road, into Natal Road, where it will enter the old Streatham Bus Garage (near the southern terminus of route 159 at Streatham Station). The bus looks as though it has been treated to a new coat of paint, and no advertisements are in evidence.
P7210009jy21

Below: RML2264 turns into the Streatham High Road, as it sets off en route for Marble Arch, operating route 159 in July. Motorist will note the speed camera just to the left of the bus front . Both photographs were taken in July. P7210014jy21

Above: RML2264 and RML892 lay over at the southern terminus of route 159, Streatham Station. The vehicles are actually at the front of the old Streatham Bus Garage, in July, with five months left for Routemasters in normal London service.
P7210007jy21

Right:
RM1280 has just turned into Natal Road from the Streatham High Road, as it approaches the Streatham Garage laying over point for the Streatham Station terminus of route 159. The photo was taken in July.
P1720018jy21

Right: RML2573 waits at traffic lights in Lower Regent Street during July. The bus is operating route 159 and is bound for Marble Arch

Below: - RMLs 2753 & 2572, both operating on route 159 are seen here outside Brixton Garage, waiting for crews, in the middle of July. There would be about four and a half months of Routemaster operation remaining when this picture was

Right: RML2375 is on the 159 in Oxford Street in August with no destination indicated, (but headed for Marble Arch).
Below: RML2759 at the same place, on the same day, is incorrectly indicated to terminate at Oxford Circus. This bus had the highest bonnet number held by Arriva.
22&24slr976285au26

Right: RML2549 makes its way down the Haymarket as it journeys to Streatham Station, on route 159 in late August.

Below: RML2375 on route 159, heads a convoy of buses along Oxford Street in late August, as it heads for distant Streatham Station.

25(25)slr976287au26&P8260014au26

Right:
RML2619 operating on route 159 during September, waits at pedestrian traffic lights in Trafalgar Square as it heads for Streatham Station . On its nearside waits a Trans Bus Trident, (TNA33384) of First, operating route 23 to Liverpool Street.
IMG1268can/s26-

Below: - RM54 pauses in Trafalgar Square, whilst operating route 159 towards Streatham Station in September. This bus has an early type body, as evidenced by the non-opening style upper deck front windows. Also in the picture are, alongside the Routemaster Trans Bus Trident 17914 of Stagecoach on route 15, and behind can be seen a 'bendy bus', Mercedes Benz Citaro 23017 on route 453.
IMG1251can/s26

Right: RML2521 operating on route 159 passes through Trafalgar Square, during September, heading West for Marble Arch.

Below: In this shot, taken in September, RM871 is on route 159 and is passing through Trafalgar Square, before heading South East for Streatham Station. The bus is a refurbished RM as shown by the hopper windows.
IMG1271&IMG1274can/s26

Left: RM548 is seen here in early October, in Oxford Street on route 159, and well on its way to its Marble Arch destination. This vehicle, which has hopper windows, has been refurbished by Marshalls.

IMG1361can113a/o6

Below: Another view of RML2521, this time in Oxford Street in October, just opposite the John Lewis store. The bus is on its way to Marble Arch, and is alongside a DVL/Wrightbus of Arriva on route 137 and a TransBus Trident of First London (TNA33362), and behind can just be seen the side view of a Mercedes Citaro Bendy Bus. IMG1364can113a/o6

Right: RML2753 in Regent Street queues to enter the crowd of buses at Oxford Circus. The bus, on route 159 in early October is bound for Marble Arch. This view shows off the welcoming open rear platform used by generations of Londoners to hop on and off.
IMG1334 can113a/o6

Below: - The photo shows RM1975 at Oxford Circus on route 159 in early October. The bus is turning out of Regent Street into Oxford Street, en route for Marble Arch. This bus was once in preservation when its nickname was 'Rory'. It seems to have sustained some damage to the front nearside roof panels since returning to passenger carrying service.
IMG1339can113a/o6

Left: RML892 outside Brixton Garage on a sunny late October day, is near the end of its run from Marble Arch to Streatham Station. A Wright Volvo B7TL (class WVL) is on the opposite side of the road on route 133 with another behind. IMG1693can116/o20

Below: - RML2545 is seen here on Westminster Bridge, with Big Ben and the Houses of Parliament behind, as it heads for Streatham Station on a beautiful day in late October. The Routemaster is followed by a Mercedes Benz Citaro 'Bendy Bus' on route 12. IMG1669can116/o20

Right: RML2619, glowing in mid November sun, swings from Westminster Bridge into Parliament Square as it heads for Marble Arch. Just behind is Stagecoach's Dennis Trident Alexander (17315) on route 53.
IMG2765can256crd/127/n14

Below: RML2521 is seen in mid November in Whitehall, en route for Streatham Station. Views behind encompass Trafalgar Square, with Nelson's Column and the National Gallery. When this photo was taken Routemasters would only be seen here on route 159 for another three weeks or so. IMG2790can256crd127/n14

Above: The photographer was waiting for a gap in the traffic to take a shot of RML2586, laying over at Marble Arch, when into the viewfinder came RM1913 with a route 9 indicator board. As it was November 14, and the first day of the new 'Heritage Routes' this was obviously an escapee from those. See below.

Right: RM1913 seen at Hyde Park Corner on November 14th. first day of the new 'Heritage' Routes, 9 & 15. The bus has been freshly painted into London Transport livery for new heritage route no. 9 which is operated by First. The 15 was to be operated by Stagecoach.

IMG2524&2523can512crd/125/n14

Above: RML2586 lays over at Marble Arch in mid November. The bus is showing signs of its long service life, and is generally travel stained and weary. Below: RML2387 looking equally travel weary and battered pulls away from the lay over point at Marble Arch, to return to Streatham. IMG2528&2526can512crd/125/n14

Above: A bevy of beautiful buses at Marble Arch in mid November. From the left are RML2636, RML2577 & RM713. Below: RML2264 passes the Marble Arch in November, as it starts its journey to Streatham. In the background is Metroline's Volvo B7TL TranBus President (VPL581) on route 390 to Archway Station.
Img2567can512crd/125/&Img2613/126n14

Above: RML2549 outside the Three Stags at the junction of Kennington Road and Lambeth Road is en route for Streatham. Below: RML892 passes road works as it approaches the junction of Kennington Road and Kennington Park Road, also bound for Streatham. Both photos were taken in late November. IMG2931&2972can512crd129/n22

Left: RM875, a refurbished RM, prepares to make the right turn from Camberwell New Road, into Kennington Park Road, at the Oval, whilst heading for Marble Arch on route 159 just two weeks before the Routemasters were finally withdrawn. The bus behind is Arriva's Daf/ Alexander DLA161 on route 59 for Euston Station. IMG3000can526crd129/n22

Below: RML2324 is in Kennington Road, at the junction with Lambeth Road, and near to the Imperial War Museum, at the end of November, with just ten days to go before Routemaster service comes to an end in London. IMG3228can512crd132/n29

Above: At the end of November, with ten days to go, RML2324, in company with Bendy Bus MA50 & TransBus Trident of London United (TLA20) is turning out of a sunny Oxford Street, into the Marble Arch roundabout system, prior to laying over near Speakers Corner.
Below: On December 7th. with only two days left to go three Routemasters are seen laying over, as if lined up for the camera, by Speaker's Corner at Marble Arch. They are RML2573, RML2264 and RM346. IMG3125can512crd131/n29&IMG3428can256crd134d7

The Penultimate Day Arrives

To avoid dangers to the large number of enthusiasts expected on the final day of Routemaster operation, it was decided to finish Routemaster services at around 2.30 pm on December 9th. This was because Brixton Garage is situated on a very busy road. As a result, the day settled on for the appearance of 'guest' buses to 'celebrate' the end of the Routemasters was the Thursday December 8th.

Above (left): Blue Triangle's RT3062 is seen here outside Lambeth Town Hall. Above (right): RML2665 is in Stagecoach livery outside Streatham Hill Station.
Below: One star of the day was RMF1254. In smart London Transport livery this front entrance Routemaster was an unusual sight outside Brixton Garage. It never worked in London until it appeared at the last day celebrations for Routemasters on route 38.
IMG3548can512crd134&IMG3466&IMG3504can512/135/d8

Left: RML2760, (the last Routemaster to be produced), is seen on December 8th. at Streatham Hill. Owned by Stagecoach and restored by them in traditional London Transport livery, it was looking very smart for this special day. IMG3516Can 512crd135/d8

Right: From the London Transport Museum and looking like a new bus, (although over 50 years old), was RM1. In London Transport livery, it is seen at the Junction of St. Matthews Road and Brixton Hill. That this is an early body is evidenced by the non opening upper deck front windows. Note too the brake vents on either side of the radiator. IMG3554Can 512crd135/d8

Left: Blue Triangle's RCL2260 is seen here at the junction of Coldharbour Lane and Brixton Road, not far from Brixton Station. The vehicle is in Green Line livery, but carries Blue Triangle's name within the 'Greenline' logo. The RCLs entered service in 1965.

IMG3570can512crd135/d8

Above Left: RTW467 on route 159, operating as a guest bus, is seen queuing in traffic opposite Lambeth Town Hall, at the junction of Coldharbour Lane and Brixton Road, in Brixton, on December 8th.
Above Right: RML2565, also operating as a guest bus on the same day, is seen here outside Brixton Garage looking rather smart in Stratford Blue livery.
Below: Arriva's RMC1453, is seen here on December 8th. looking very smart, outside Brixton Garage and overtaking RML2573. RMC1453 was the first production RMC. It entered service in August 1962.

IMG3585&IMG3599&IMG3591can512crd135/d8

Above: TD895 of Ensign Bus and RML2387 make the right turn from the Streatham High Road into Natal Road, to lay over, after arriving at Streatham Station. Below: RM29 and RT624 outside the old Streatham Bus Garage. Both photos were taken on the penultimate day of Routemaster service on the 159.
IMG3646&IMG3694can512crd136/d8

The Final Day - December 9th

Not only the last day for Routemasters on the 159, but the final curtain for the Routemaster in London, and for the open rear platform half cab bus, (with the minor exception of some dozen refurbished Routemasters operating a restricted 'Heritage' service on routes 9 & 15).

Above: RM 54, seen here near Streatham Hill Station sets off for its last journey to Marble Arch. Although RM2217 was to be the last official Routemaster in service, in fact RM54 ran the last normal Routemaster service from Streatham to Marble Arch and back to Streatham. IMG3707can128crd137/d9

Right: VLA168 - (a Volvo B7TL with an Alexander Dennis ALX400 body), waits in Natal Road, before operating one of the first non-Routemaster journeys to Marble Arch. The bus is still showing an 'Out of Service' indicator, as it waits to enter the old Streatham Garage lay over point, prior to its first run 'in anger'. IMG3715can128crd137d9

Above: RML2619 and RML895 at Streatham Station. By this stage, (around 11.20am), all Routemasters returning to Streatham Station were, instead of turning round at the old Streatham Garage, continuing straight on Southwards, like the two above, towards some Routemaster Valhalla. The only buses setting off towards Marble Arch were now the new VLAs. IMG3725can128crd137/d9

Above: RML2521, the photographer's favourite, still with its 'Zeno' graffiti, stops opposite Streatham Ice Rink, the final stop, to disgorge its passengers for the very last time. This included the photographer, who took his last ride on this bus, on this final day of Routemasters. A moment later, followed by RM1145, she would drive away to destinations, and a future unknown. How many passengers has she carried in her working life of over forty years, and on what different routes, and in what different places has she served, and what will become of her? IMG3740can128crd137/d9

Above: RM54, the actual last Routemaster, arrives at Streatham. The 'official' last Routemaster, RM2217, freshly painted for the occasion, and gleaming, can be seen arriving below, surrounded by enthusiasts. IMG3804&3811can256crd138/d9

Above: RM2217, the last (standard length) RM built, and now the Official Last Routemaster, struggles through the throng of enthusiasts who've come to bid their favourite bus farewell. A sad moment but tinged with a shared feeling of gladness to be at this momentous occasion. Below: RM2217 makes its last farewell, as it passes slowly into the dark depths of Brixton Garage, watched by hundreds of Routemaster fans, who can't really believe it's all over.

IMG3815&3822can128crd138/d9

LAST WORDS (by the Author)

At the time of writing all of the Routemasters withdrawn during 2005 had been found a home, none had been scrapped. Some had gone to preservationists, some were sold abroad, and some were taken by bus operators for special services.

This would seem a good time to pay tribute to all those enthusiasts who preserve and restore old buses. They commit many hours and much energy, and often large sums of money, to ensure that old buses remain to be seen and enjoyed by future generations. In particular I would like to pay tribute to the late Norman Myers, who saved so many old British Buses from passing to the scrap-yard. Thanks to him, many of them are now still in existence, and are there for us all to enjoy.

Acknowledgements:
Thanks are extended to Colin Curtis OBE., for his kind permission to use a quotation from his book. Also to my Partner, Shirley Cantello, for her support and patience during the many long hours that were spent by me, in London taking photographs, and at the computer putting this book together. Also, thanks to my friend Dave North, who gave me so much invaluable help with computer matters, and with photo - manipulation. JMW.

INDEX OF BUSES APPEARING IN THIS BOOK

(contd on page 152)

(contd from p.151)

Non-Routemasters (Classics):

Non-Routemasters (Modern):